To Darling Lauren
Such special Memories

"When one tugs at a single thing in nature,
he finds it attached to the
rest of the world."

John Muir

First Edition
Library of Congress
Control Number: 2008902194
ISBN13: 978-0-9708104-6-5 (hardcover)

12 11 10 09   7 6 5 4 3 2

Printed in China

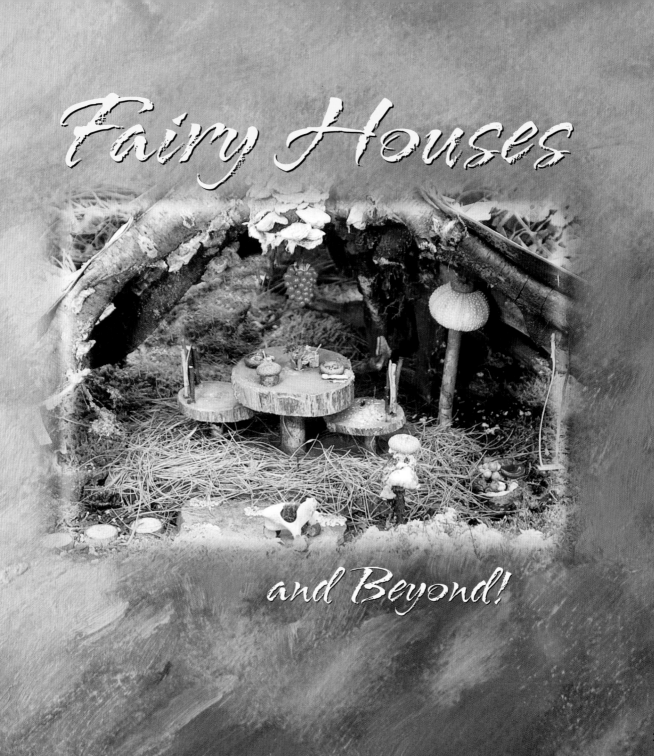

Fairy Houses

and Beyond!

Exploring the woods on a coastal island, I discovered my first fairy houses. These small dwellings were scattered along the path, tucked amongst tree roots and rocks. Built only from natural materials, they seemed almost hidden by the morning mist.

Inspired, I gathered sticks and fallen pine brush to build a fairy house of my own. Enjoying the serenity, I pondered using bark for the roof and dried grass for the floor. As sunlight filtered through the misty canopy, nature's enchantment transported me back to my youth. If only someone had introduced me to this activity when I was a child.

Ideas flowed like breezes blowing off the ocean. My imagination soared as the rustling leaves above seemed to whisper, "Story...story." What if I were to write and illustrate a book about building fairy houses? The story could introduce this delightful activity to children everywhere. What a fun way to appreciate nature's wonders!

The success of *The Fairy Houses Series*™ has fostered many workshops and community events with families building these whimsical habitats. Many of these creations have been photographed by my husband, Barry. A visual tour of these houses can be enjoyed in our first co-authored book, *Fairy Houses ... Everywhere!* This, our second book, showcases photographs of fairy houses as they continue to evolve ... and amaze!

Tracy Kane

Contents

Stories Shared

Through my travels and interactions with people across the country, I discovered that fairy house building is a catalyst for so many things: It is a way to explore and participate in the wonder of nature; to bring people closer together as they collaborate in an activity with nature; to provide an opportunity for children of all ages to create, invent and learn. I am delighted to share a few of the magical stories that have been passed on to me ...

Grandma's Garden

A granddaughter was staying with her grandmother as they awaited a new arrival in the family. The little girl was distracted, wondering when her parents would return and whether she would have a new baby sister. As a way to help pass time Grandma suggested watching the movie, Kristen's Fairy House. Afterwards, the granddaughter wanted to go outside and build a fairy house, like Kristen did.

They made great partners and were soon swept up in the excitement of creating an inviting structure for the fairies. It was triangular in shape and set against a tree. They worked in tandem, making soft beds from fallen petals and delicious meals of blueberries in seashells. They hoped to entice the fairies to spend the night at their newly created house.

Early next morning, the child awoke remembering her mother was in the hospital and there would soon be a new baby in the family. She rose quickly and went to wake up her grandmother.

"Grandma," she said earnestly. "We have to go outside and add a fairy nursery to our house!"

Librarian's Tale

A librarian in Tucson, Arizona chose the book, Fairy Houses, for her summer reading program. Her students were very inspired by the story and asked if they could build fairy houses outside on the library grounds.

The Librarian looked wistfully out the window at the arid landscape and said, "You know, they have to be constructed totally from natural materials."

Nodding their heads, they replied enthusiastically, "We know that!"

"All right, all right!" she responded. "If you bring in the natural supplies with you next week, we'll build houses for the fairies."

And they did! They brought in colorful desert rocks, dried cholla cactus stems, corn husks and cotton balls. One boy even spent the week brushing his dog and saving the fur. He wanted a soft floor for the fairies to land on!

Lost on the Trail

Several families decided to take a day hike in the White Mountains of New Hampshire. The weather was spectacular, rewarding the hikers with beautiful views. It was a splendid time, until they began heading down the mountain and realized they were lost. Daylight was fading and the White Mountains grow cold at night, even in the summer. The hikers decided to send two adults ahead to find the right trail. The others would stay where they were, as the children were tired and spirits were sinking fast. One mother, in an effort to distract the youngsters, suggested they build fairy houses. Majestic trees and an abundance of forest materials provided a perfect setting. Soon everyone was absorbed in creating a neighborhood of woodland fairy houses.

When the scouts returned, the families were so completely engaged in this activity they hardly noticed an additional hiker had joined them. He explained the trail they needed was just ten minutes away and they could easily make it down the mountain before dark.

However, they now had a new problem - the children wanted to stay and continue building fairy houses!

Enchantment at School

When a teacher in Florida read *The Fairy Houses Series*™ to her second grade class, they enthusiastically came up with a plan. The class decided to construct a fairy village on the school's property and then write a story about it. The children collected native materials from home and chose a location amongst low shrubbery at the edge of the playground.

As they were adding the finishing touches to their eclectic dwellings, the sky darkened and a squall moved in rapidly. The children noticed a small golden patch in the sky, flickering up and down like a wave amidst the dark ominous clouds. It was a gathering of Monarch butterflies heading their way!

To the children's delight, just before the rain started falling, the butterflies found their fairy houses and flew inside to take shelter.

"It was a moment of enchantment," recalled the teacher. "I now have a class of true believers!"

Fairy Houses can be created in many

Different Environments

Woodland

Beach

Meadow

Mountain

Tropics

Tundra

Fairy Villages

Fairy Houses are evolving into
fairy neighborhoods and communities

Coastal Village

Medieval Castle

Medieval Village

Fairy
Art Colony

Theater

Opera Box

Cabaret Dinner Theater

Art

Supplies

Pottery

Painting

Music

Harp

Drums

Orchestra

31

Spas & Relaxation

Even fairies need a place
to contemplate nature's
wonders.

Retreats & Meditation

Dining

Living

Sleeping

Playtime

Archeological Dig

Summer Solstice

Camera in hand and thousands of pictures of fairy houses later, I still find the variety of fairy house designs astounding. What began with individual, rustic habitats has grown to include fairy villages, castles, lighthouses—even art colonies!

I find it remarkable when three generations form a creative team; parents, grandparents and children all weaving their talents into the creative building process. These are precious, memorable moments I wish to capture, when families bond and explore the natural world.

As I crouch under the branches of a tree, I am rewarded with a fairy's-eye view. I chuckle and wonder at the whimsical touches of the interiors, some clearly taking hours to design and construct. My thoughts are interrupted as I feel a tug at my elbow. "I have a visitor," a child's voice announces excitedly. "Come and see the grasshopper that has moved into my house! Maybe he likes the berries I left in the acorn cap for the fairies to eat."

Their joy is contagious. Grinning broadly, I dutifully follow, ready to be a good listener … and begin to click away.

I realize there is no limit to the exciting possibilities.

Barry Kane

Winter Solstice

Award-Winning Inspiration from Tracy Kane

The Fairy Houses Series®

Connecting Families and Nature...with a pinch of Fairy magic!

The Illustrated Series

Fairy Houses
by Tracy Kane
ISBN10 0-9708104-5-8
ISBN13: 978-0-9708104-5-8
$15.95 US, 40 Pages

What happens if you build
a house for the fairies to
live in?

Will they come to visit?

"Top 10 Pick" Children's Book Sense - American Booksellers Assn.

Kristen's Fairy House - DVD
UPC 884277000020 ISBN13: 978-09708104-9-6
DVD 40 mins. $19.95 US

What is the mystery of the small habitats
built in the woods by visiting children?

Join Kristen on a unique and
wonderful adventure of discovery!

As seen on National Public Television!
Parents' Choice Gold Award!

Fairy Boat
by Tracy Kane
ISBN10: 0-9708104-7-4
ISBN13: 978-0-9708104-7-2
$15.95 US, 40 Pages

What happens if you
build a boat for fairies?

Can the fairies save Fairy Boat
on its perilous journey?

"Children's Book Sense" pick - American Booksellers Association

Fairy Flight
by Tracy Kane
ISBN10: 0-9708104-2-3
ISBN13: 978-0-9708104-2-7
$15.95 US, 40 Pages

Are butterflies really
fairies in disguise?

Follow a very special
butterfly migration to its
wonderful conclusion!

The Photo Series

Fairy Houses ... Everywhere!
by Barry & Tracy Kane

ISBN10: 0-9708104-4-X
ISBN13: 978-0-9708104-4-1
$14.95 US, 56 Pages

Have you ever seen
a Fairy House?

Presenting a photographic tour of fairy houses.
From rustic habitats to fairy mansions, these are creations
of families, gardeners and nature lovers ... everywhere!

Fairy Houses and Beyond!
by Barry & Tracy Kane

ISBN13: 978-0-9708104-6-5
$15.95 US, 62 Pages

Have you ever seen
a Fairy Village?

Fairy Houses are evolving. Discover fairy neighborhoods,
villages and even art colonies! Built with natural materials
and a pinch of creativity ... the possibilities are infinite!

The Mystery Series

A Fairy Houses Mystery

FOREST SECRETS

by Tracy Kane
& Kelly Sanders

ISBN: 978-0-976628-91-0
$14.95 US, 126 Pages

Kate is thrilled when she realizes that her new home borders an enchanted forest. Nothing is more fascinating to Kate than the wonders of nature.

She meets Luke Carver, a real nature geek. Together they discover a fairy house hidden in the trunk of a tree. Inside, they find a mysterious clue. Who built the fairy house, and why? What other secrets does the forest hold?

As Luke and Kate investigate the mystery, they learn that the woods is in danger. They are determined to save the forest, but how? Where's the fairy dust when you need it?

Visit our award-winning website
www.fairyhouses.com
for inspiring photos, events and downloads

Also from *Tracy Kane* ...

The Magic of Color

by Tracy Kane

ISBN10: 0-9766289-0-2
ISBN13: 978-0-9766289-0-3
$17.95 US, 40 Pages

"Children's Book Sense" pick - American Booksellers Assoc.

Can you imagine an Earth without color?
No blue sky, green grass or brilliant red sunsets?

Two tribes exist peacefully on an island in a world of black and white. A dramatic event occurs creating two colors that transforms their lives. When a third color appears on the mountain peak both tribes set off on an adventure to claim this dazzling new treasure.

Their journey leads them to a startling encounter and they discover a new world more wonderful than any they could imagine.

A combination of art, color and cultures make this a truly memorable story on many levels.

www.magicofcolor.com

Light-Beams
PUBLISHING

10 Toon Lane Lee, NH 03861
www.light-beams.com
1.800.397.7641
info@light-beams.com